A GOOD TIME
TO BE THE CHURCH

A GOOD TIME TO BE THE CHURCH

A Conversation with
Bishop H. George Anderson

Augsburg
MINNEAPOLIS

A GOOD TIME TO BE THE CHURCH
A Conversation with Bishop H. George Anderson

Scripture quotations are from the New Revised Standard Version Bible, copyright © 1989 by the Division of Christian Education of the National Council of the Churches of Christ in the U.S.A. and used by permission.

Some of the material in this book was adapted from the *Lutheran* and from *The Anderson Interviews*, by Lutheran Vespers.

Cover photo courtesy of the *Lutheran*
Cover design by David Meyer
Text design by James Satter

Anderson, H. George (Hugh George), 1932-
    A good time to be the church : a conversation with Bishop
H. George Anderson.
        p.   cm.
    Includes bibliographical references.
    ISBN 0-8066-3525-8 (alk. paper)
    1. Church. 2. Lutheran Church—Doctrines. 3. Anderson,
H. George (Hugh George), 1932-   . I. Title.
BV600.2.A495 1996
284.1'35—dc21   96-51960
                                                             CIP

The paper used in this publication meets the minimum requirements of American National Standard for Information Sciences—Permanence of Paper for Printed Library Materials, ANSI Z329.48-1984.

Manufactured in the U.S.A.   AF 9-3525

01   00   99   98   97   2   3   4   5   6   7   8   9   10

CONTENTS

1

A GOOD TIME
TO BE THE CHURCH

FOR A LONG TIME, Lutherans never made the Big Top of American church life. The histories of religion in America told the stories of the Great Awakenings, the Evangelical Revival, the Social Gospel, and other major movements without mentioning Lutherans at all. We were relegated to sideshow status, usually getting a separate chapter along with Catholics and Jews, all grouped together as "immigrant faiths."

Since World War II all that has changed. Now Lutherans are emerging from their ethnic isolation and joining the mainline denominations —just as the mainline seems to be going down the tubes! It is as though we had been amassing our life savings in order to join the rich and famous on an ocean cruise, only to discover when we buy our tickets that the name of our ship is *Titanic*.

During the 1990s, at least fourteen major books have been written on the misery of the mainline denominations. "Mainline" used to describe the church bodies that dominated American culture. Now one writer has proposed that we should change their title to "oldline" —or maybe even "sideline."

At least three forces have pushed the mainline to the margins. The first is the growth of the Evangelical wing of American Protestantism. Not only have these denominations grown numerically, but they have used TV and other media to their advantage. Through groups like the Moral Majority and the Christian Coalition they have captured the attention of America on many hot public issues. They are a new force in American religious life.

Second, many other Americans are opting out of the organized church. They have been called "believers, not belongers." There used to be a sharp line between churchgoing believers and the unbelievers, but now there is a growing gray area of people who neither belong to traditional denominations nor reject religion altogether. A recent survey of Presbyterian baby boomers found that the largest categories were "moderately active Presbyterians" (29 percent) and the "uninvolved but religious" (21 percent). The problem was that in actual beliefs the two groups barely differed!

Already about one-half of all Protestants change denominations at least once, and they probably don't feel the need to add or subtract a single doctrine in the process. Even within the denominations, I suspect, lifestyle rather than religion is the organizing principle of most lives. They are not "rooted in the gospel"; they are rooted in a social class or a lifestyle, and the gospel is an ornament they wear, like a gold cross around their neck.

The third great change on the American religious scene is the arrival of major world religions. The number of Muslims in the United States is now about equal to the number of Episcopalians, and by 2000 there will be more Muslims than Jews in this country. Right now there are as many mosques in our country as there are ELCA congregations. The armed services have announced that they will soon be augmenting the traditional Protestant–Catholic–Jewish pattern of military chaplaincies by adding a fourth category—Muslim.

What, then, shall we say to these things? What do these changes mean for the future of Christianity? Are we going to witness the end of the Christian era, or the end of organized religion, or at least the death of denominations? More directly, what do they mean for the future of our church? A closer look at our situation will reveal some heartening insights.

Nostalgia isn't what it used to be.

The good old days really weren't so great after all. When we think about the way things really ought to be in the church, we tend to long for the days when pews were full, mission congregations were sprouting up all over, and every congregation met its financial goals 100 percent.

When were those days? Most people would

say, "In the 1950s—that's when the church really had it all together." In fact, the 1950s are often viewed as a time of religious revival.

Well, I'm old enough to remember those days. They were dominated by pressures of the Cold War. Russia had beaten us in the race to develop space technology. We were still reeling from the attacks on the church by Senator Joe McCarthy, who claimed that one out of every three Protestant clergy was a Communist sympathizer. It is no wonder that most people felt the proper label for this time was "the age of anxiety."

Many observers in those years lamented the shallowness of church membership, claiming that people were joining because IBM or some other corporation expected them to, as a symbol of corporate involvement in the community. Some experts attributed the attendance to nervousness over the Cold War. Roy Eckardt, in his contemporary analysis called *The Surge of Piety in America* (1958), described the revival as an upsurge of interest in religion rather than genuine religion itself.

In short, despite the statistics, religious commitment in those days was pretty shallow, like the roots of the seed that fell on sandy soil. Many theologians warned that the revival was more shadow than substance, and that it could wilt away as dramatically as it had flourished. Subsequent history proved those skeptics right.

Martin Marty could have been describing this era when he said, "There are no golden ages, only yellow ones."

We are always at a crossroads.

Henrik Kraemer, a Dutch expert on missions, wrote fifty years ago, "Strictly speaking, one ought to say that the church is always in a state of crisis, and that its greatest shortcoming is that it is only occasionally aware of it." Today we are certainly aware of the crisis—perhaps in an exaggerated way. Loren Mead has written:

> We are at the front edges of the greatest trans-formation of the Church that has occurred for 1,600 years. It is by far the greatest change that the Church has ever experienced in America; it may eventually make the transfor-mation of the Reformation look like a ripple in a pond.

> I really doubt that the membership woes of five or six U.S. denominations will amount to much more than a minor skin irritation on the body of Christ—now spread over six continents and doing very well on many of them.

> Of course, that doesn't help those of us who are experiencing the stresses of these changes.

To us the threats are real, the pangs excruciating. We don't like to see our beloved church falling behind or losing out. We question our own ability; we wonder if we are the problem—or at least if our church is the problem.

But there have been other moments of crisis in the last years. I lived in the South during the 1950s, when the public schools were desegregated and our local pastors had to take a stand. Some of them lost their jobs. Others saw their congregations split. Most of you remember the family stress caused by generational differences regarding the Vietnam War. It was not an easy time to minister, especially when institutions like the Church were under direct attack.

What decade has been without its challenges and stress? Desegregation in the 1950s, Vietnam in the 1960s, charismatic renewal and historical criticism in the 1970s, merger in the 1980s, human sexuality in the 1990s. There is always an issue, always a threat to unity, always human pride and stubbornness to make a mountain out of a molehill. What will our worries look like to the next generation?

God never lets the church stand still.

If you survey the long history of Christianity, you will find that every time the Church found success, something bad happened to it. For example, it had no sooner climbed out of persecution and become the official church of the Roman Empire than the barbarians sacked Rome and ended that triumph. During the Middle Ages, the Church again created an empire for itself and humbled the mightiest rulers of Europe, only to crack apart because of inner corruption and decay. Revolutions in the nineteenth and twentieth centuries destroyed the culture Protestantism that arose in the wake of Catholic Christendom, and, on a smaller scale, the unrest of the 1960s interrupted the religious revival of the 1950s.

It seems that God just won't let the Church settle down and enjoy its triumphs. Every time we want to linger on the Mount of Transfiguration, God pushes us off the scenic viewpoint and lands us back in some valley. It's just like walking: if you stand still, you are perfectly balanced, but you don't get anywhere. But if someone—maybe God—gives you a little push, you have to put a foot out to keep from falling. From your point of view it was a fall avoided, but from another point of view, you took a step forward.

Someone has wisely written that college faculties are all in favor of progress; it's just change that they don't like. The reason is that "progress" sounds like we're getting something more than we had. "Change" often implies that we will lose something important or precious to us.

How can we keep in mind that old truth that we sometimes have to let go of the old in order to grasp the new? In theological terms, are we ready to forgo immortality in order to experience resurrection? It is exactly the times of hardship and stress that force us to look beyond our own resources and to depend on God. This time of uncertainty need not be the prelude to disaster. It can become the occasion for powerful spiritual renewal.

We are not dealing with a problem, but with a mess.

Problems are specific and individual. They can be attacked one by one. When you solve one, you move on to another. That's the way we have been looking at stewardship, for example, or evangelism.

But if Loren Mead is right, we are like that woodsman in the fairy tale who discovers that every chip that flies from the trunk is replaced by two new ones. We can't deal with things one at a time because all our problems are inter-connected.

But even the biggest messes hold promise. If you translate "mess" into Greek, you'll come out with a word like "chaos," and God certainly did well with chaos the first time around. After all, didn't chaos itself form the matrix for God's creation of heaven and earth? One of the cutting edges of science today is the study of chaos because it is the great new frontier for discovery.

Science has selected those problems, such as atomic structure and astronomy, that display regular, uniform, predictable action. But there is a lot in nature, like weather and behavior, that won't yield to that sort of analysis, as any prediction of next weekend's weather will demonstrate. Only recently have scientists begun to use what they call "chaos theory" to address these complex and interrelated dynamic systems. Chaos theory rests on the discovery that, underneath apparently random behavior, there is often one or more "attractors" that define it.

So what, if any, patterns underline the mess that the church is in? Let's start with the demographic shift. The movement of population, of course, is nothing new. In fact, the frontier posed the first great problem of population migration in America—a problem that continued for two centuries. Later, the migration from the North and Midwest to the South and Southwest brought Lutherans from areas where they were numerous to areas where they were sparse. But their loyalty was high, and they came bounding up to our mission doors like retrievers with letters of transfer in their teeth.

Now, however, that demographic flow has been overlaid by two other major shifts—the mobility of two-income families seeking work, and the increase of multiculturalism. When Lutherans land in Louisiana or L.A., they aren't coming from some small town or farm where denominational affiliation was predetermined by bloodlines. They have already been in the military, or moved to the city, or worked for a company that had moved them a couple of times. They are trying to raise a family and don't have a lot of time to put in on church councils or Sunday school teaching.

As a result, they often appear less committed than their predecessors to our denomination or even to congregational life. The other new complicating factor is the pluralism that I mentioned at the beginning of this survey. Since the 1960s we have seen a testing of all the "givens" of American society, from the quality of our school system to the integrity of our government. Persons who have been ignored or marginalized by our culture have asserted their right to be heard. Where the old truths did not recognize them, new truths have been proposed. The result is a cultural transition that may outlast all of us. As a consequence, we live in unsettled, fluid times.

We experience this factor negatively as a loss of traditional faith, but it can also be seen as an opportunity to provide direction to a seeking generation. Our society is in a molten state, when decisive action can have its greatest effect. Openness to new religious experience offers us a chance to reach persons whose parents would never have considered the Lutheran church. In fact, this openness puts us at the threshold of possibilities far greater than any we can imagine.

Present trends never continue.

Those who know me may remember my doubts about predicting the future. I learned that caution from listening to a great church historian, Dr. Kenneth Scott Latourette, reply to reporters who asked him, "As a historian, what do you predict . . . ?" He always answered, "As a historian, I know that predictions seldom come true."

Why can the experts who make predictions be so wildly wrong? Because they are experts—

knowing a great deal about a tiny fraction of this complicated world. Thomas Watson, the chairman of IBM, knew a lot more about computers than most of the rest of us did in 1943, but he was so fixed on the idea of size and number crunching that he never dreamed of miniaturization and the possibility of word processing.

Furthermore, history is woven out of human freedom, and no matter how large your statistical sample you cannot cancel out freedom's surprising effects. History is the kingdom of newness, the place where the creative Spirit of God continually is "doing a new thing." Someone has said, "If you want to hear God laugh, tell God your plans."

Although we cannot predict the future, there is one thing we can be sure of:

God's Church will endure to the end.

When things looked bleak for the infant Reformation, Martin Luther assured his coworkers that God would defend God's own cause. God had said that the gates of hell would not prevail against the church, and God would see to it that the promise was kept. Our own concern, said Luther, should simply be to remain faithful to God's invincible cause. Granted that the Church will survive, how about our own tradition? Many commentators claim that denominations are a thing of the past.

I think that is highly unlikely. Anyone who has tried to close a congregation or move a graveyard knows that religious institutions are very durable.

Denominational structures are like seashells. They are created, bit by bit, as houses for living organisms, but they can outlast their founders and become a home for hermit crabs and other life that has no connection with the original builders. The question is not whether denominations will survive, but whether they will continue to grow and change or just become hollow structures harboring nothing more than the sound of distant surf.

Our denominations were built around great causes—foreign missions, education, home missions, and the care of the aged and orphans—urgent needs that congregations could not address alone. The issue for our time is whether Christians still feel that these, or other, great causes demand their loyalty and cooperation. Otherwise, the only role for denominations is to facilitate pastoral mobility and administer pension funds.

I believe that there are still great causes, in addition to those of the past, that powerfully motivate us. Think of Lutheran World Relief and all the outpouring of money, food, and quilts that it has evoked. Think of the Hunger Appeal—raising $12 million last year to feed people around the world. Disaster Relief . . . and I could go on.

But do you notice that these causes are ones that any caring organization could adopt? The Red Cross could do them. Is there anything left that only the Church is called to do? I think there is.

We do not face a spiritual desert, but a spiritual jungle.

In 1965, *Time* magazine ran its first cover without a picture on it. It was stark black, with three words: IS GOD DEAD? The "God is dead" movement expressed the triumph of secular thought over traditional religion. But its consequences have been surprising.

The same *Time* magazine that asked about God being dead in the 1960s ran a cover story on angels in 1994. The 1990s are crowded with gods new and old. Exotic blends of New Age notions, palm reading, belief in angels, astrology—and much more—compete with popular interpretations of Native American religion, revivals of Gregorian chant, Hindu meditation, and Zen Buddhism. They bring to mind the words of G. K. Chesterton, who said that when people stop believing in God, they do not believe in nothing; they believe in anything.

The lead article in the November 28, 1994, issue of *Newsweek* was titled "In Search of the Sacred." It concludes with a quote from an anthropologist who observes, "People feel they want something they've lost, and they don't remember what it is they've lost. But it has left a gaping hole." It sounds a lot like St. Augustine's famous line, "O God, you have created us for yourself, and our hearts are restless until they find their rest in you."

Although it is true that many of our contemporaries are spiritually hungry, it does not follow that they will automatically respond to our message. Their quest may be for a different gospel, one that is self-affirming and privatistic. It is not a made-to-order receptacle for Christianity, but a counterreligion that has its demonic side. It is here that we must summon our best theological analysis in order to address these real spiritual needs—but not necessarily on their own terms.

What people *want* is comfort, security, and to be left alone. What people *need* is service, sacrifice, and being brought together.

It is our task, our challenge, to explain what's wrong, to diagnose this illness—this hunger that doesn't go away, but only gnaws more deeply—and at the same time to show that it is possible, in this world and under the stresses and suspicions of our time, to live in community. We can offer the Living Bread that satisfies the hungry heart. We have the opportunity to demonstrate that, in Christ, the dividing walls have been broken down, "so that through the church the wisdom of God in its rich variety might be made known . . ." (Ephesians 3:10).

Bread for the hungry heart.

I believe that there are four great themes we have to bring from our tradition that especially speak to the needs of our time—both for those within the church and for those spiritual seekers outside:

- We are empowered for a life of daily transformation based on our baptism.

- We live simultaneously as saints and sinners.

- Each one of us is called to use our unique gifts in service to God and humanity.

- We live and witness in the power of the Word.

In subsequent chapters we will explore each of these themes to see what they mean to us individually and as a church. These are some of the unique gifts we have to bring to spiritually hungry people in our world.

God has given us this challenge.
God has given us the power to meet it.
It is a good time to be the church.

FOR GROUP DISCUSSION

If your group has not had time to read the chapter beforehand, give them some time to read it silently now. Discuss the following questions.

1. What are the major changes in our society that most affect your congregation? our denomination?

2. Do you feel there was a "golden age" for your congregation or denomination?

3. How is your congregation affected by demographic shifts or pluralism?

4. What signs of spiritual hunger do you see in our society?

5. What do you see as the major challenges facing our church?

6. What are the signs of hope you see for our church?

7. What did you find most interesting or helpful in this chapter?

❅

You may wish to celebrate your discussion by singing a hymn like one of the following:

LBW 228, 229 *A Mighty Fortress Is Our God**
LBW 365 *Built on a Rock*
LBW 369 *The Church's One Foundation*
LBW 393 *Rise, Shine, You People!*
LBW 476 *Have No Fear, Little Flock*
WOV 753 *You Are the Seed***

* LBW stands for the *Lutheran Book of Worship* (Minneapolis: Lutheran Church in America, the American Lutheran Church, the Evangelical Lutheran Church of Canada, and the Lutheran Church—Missouri Synod, 1978).

** WOV stands for *With One Voice: A Lutheran Resource for Worship* (Minneapolis: Augsburg Fortress, 1995).

※

Close with this or another prayer:

Gracious Father, we pray for your holy catholic Church. Fill it with all truth and peace. Where it is corrupt, purify it; where it is in error, direct it; where it is in need, provide for it; where it is divided, reunite it; for the sake of Jesus Christ, your Son and Savior. [1]

2

WALKING IN
NEWNESS OF LIFE

BAPTISM IS NOT A TEN-MINUTE CEREMONY that happens to babies. It takes a lifetime to complete. Martin Luther called baptism "the daily garment which the Christian is to wear all the time." That is, the pattern of our Christian life comes from the continuous arc of baptism—being brought low, washed, and then raised up. Every day is a new experience of that cycle: recognizing our sin, remembering that we are baptized as children of God, and then being invigorated by the assurance of forgiveness.

In baptism we discover that our relationship to God is not based on what we do, but on what God in Christ has done. The ground of our relationship to God is mercy and forgiveness rather than justice. So each day we need to remind ourselves of God's mercy and forgiveness.

This merciful basis gives us the courage to admit our sin rather than hiding or denying it. This is a cleansing act that really changes the way we are in the world, the way we behave. It is not just a legal change; it transforms us— though that change is episodic and incomplete.

Have you ever watched distance runners as they struggle through the middle part of a marathon? Now and then, when they begin to feel the pressure, they pick up a cup of water from the sidelines and take a few gulps or splash it over their heads. That is a powerful metaphor for baptism—as repeated refreshment along the way.

Some Christians think of the new life in Christ as a higher spiritual plateau. But most of us find it difficult to sustain that "spiritual high." We feel like the muddy boy who came home crying to his mother because "the puddles kept sneaking up on me." So we keep coming back to God, relying on the fact that in our baptism God called us by name before we were able to speak. Surely the one who loved us while we were yet sinners loves us still.

The apostle Paul knew the same struggle in his life. One minute he lamented that he could not do the things he wanted to do, but he did the very things he hated. And the next minute he remembered that if God was powerful enough to raise Christ from the dead, God could also renew a sinner's life (Romans 7:14—8:17).

Baptism also involves renouncing "the devil and all his works and ways." This is not just archaic language, but offers a vital insight. Much of modern stress and conflict is a type of bondage: to a lifestyle (so that we need to work two jobs and acquire more things) or to a demanding spouse (so that we become codependent or can't go to church or get out of an abusive relationship) or to uncritical nationalism ("my country right or wrong"). This replacement of the true God by something less is demonic in the sense that some force less than God has taken over our lives. Baptism begins the process of setting us free from these forms of bondage to false gods.

So baptism stays with us all our days. And when death has put an end to our sinning, it still cannot put an end to our baptism. The same God who called us by name in baptism will then call us forth like Lazarus from the tomb (John 11:34-44). John Ylvisaker's hymn *I Was There to Hear Your Borning Cry* concludes with a delightful reference to this resurrection promise of God:

> When the evening gently closes in
> and you shut your weary eyes,
> I'll be there as I have always been
> with just one more surprise.

From Luther's Small Catechism:

What then is the significance of such a baptism with water? Answer: It signifies that daily the old person in us with all our sins and evil desires is to be drowned through sorrow for sin and repentance, and that daily a new person is to come forth and rise up to live before God in righteousness and purity forever.

Where is this written?

St. Paul says in Romans 6:3-4, "Do you not know that all of us who have been baptized into Christ Jesus were baptized into his death? Therefore we have been buried with him by baptism into death, so that, just as Christ was raised from the dead by the glory of the Father, so we too might walk in newness of life."

Bishop Anderson, what does your own baptism mean for you?

When I was six weeks old, Frances and Reuben Anderson came to check out the baby they were told was going to be theirs by adoption. Unfortunately, I was suffering from jaundice when they arrived, and as they described it later, I was scrawny and yellow-looking. But, thanks be to God, they said, "We'll take him anyway." They waited another month until my condition was better, and then brought me home.

I often look back on that first decision, and I think how like God's grace that was. There I was, pretty undesirable, and not very good-looking, and yet they decided at that moment to intervene in my young life, and from there on, my sixty-four years have been totally different from what they might have been.

Because of adoption I entered into a wonderful childhood, baptized in my grandmother's church, and from that time on a child of God, but also a child of loving parents who personified that grace of God for me.

Some Christians seem to think of baptism mainly as "fire insurance"—that is, because I'm baptized, I know I'll go to heaven when I die. How can we transcend that meaning?

This is a half-truth that lots of people are satisfied with, and then they miss the other truth that baptism is also for each day. Martin Luther saw baptism not just as assurance of heaven after death, but as a life of daily forgiveness and drowning of the Old Adam and the strength to begin another day and try again to be a servant of God.

Many people today don't think of themselves as being particularly sinful or under the wrath of God. How do we talk about Baptism with them?

When Paul at the beginning of Romans talks about the wrath of God, he doesn't mean that some people will be battered over the head by God. He talks about the whole world being subject to futility. I think that's how people experience the wrath of God—as a sense of futility, as meaninglessness. And people need to understand that behind their sense of meaninglessness there's a God-relationship involved.

Of course, people still experience feelings of guilt, maybe not today so much around issues of sex, but often about how they treated their parents or their children. So people need the power of the gospel to address that guilt as well as the deep issue of meaninglessness.

How in congregations can we help people be more aware of the daily meaning of their baptism?

One of the ways is for us to study again the need and practice of prayer. There is a celebratory aspect of the Christian life, a giving thanks and a rejoicing in the present day. But there is also looking at our past, engaging in self-examination, putting our life up against the pattern of discipleship we see revealed in the Bible and in the life of Christ. I need to ask, "What in my past is prohibiting me from doing what I need to do today? Who can't I talk to because I'm nursing a grudge? What am I limited from doing by unresolved conflicts?" These questions can show us ways in which we are in bondage. I also think we could make better use of the confessional prayers and also the service of the affirmation of baptism.

How do you remind yourself that you are baptized?

Well, that goes so deep. After a while it's not a matter anymore of reminding yourself. It's the way I start praying by expecting that I can bring all my guilt and feelings to God, confident that this will not break the relationship with God, but rather restore it.

I remember one incident from my childhood when my brother and I got into some mischief and lied about it. I remember running into the kitchen half-dressed—I was getting ready for bed—and telling my mother what had really happened. It was a way of clarifying our relationship with each other. I just had to do it.

Likewise, my wife and I have had an agreement that we will not let an argument go on overnight. We settle our differences each day. In the same way, living out the meaning of our baptism, we renew daily our relationship with God.

How has the assurance that you're baptized freed you to act in the world?

It helps me to understand Luther's advice to "sin boldly" because the promise connected with baptism allows us to make decisions knowing we have a forgiving God. Some decisions we have to make are pretty clear, but with some others, one has to say, "I don't know. There's just no clear answer, no clear way I can move forward." In that kind of situation baptism allows me to see God as present in the decision, more like a coach helping me get through the race than like a judge who's going to determine whether I came in first, second, or last. Baptism doesn't simply let you walk out of a marriage or other relationship; but it tells you that it is worth struggling with the real issues because God is present with you in the decision.

In addition to these personal aspects of Baptism, what is the communal meaning?

For me the most wonderful moment in the service of Baptism is when the pastor turns with the child to the congregation and the people say, "We welcome you." That is the real meaning of Baptism. That's where I see the community as so important. If this child is to understand that God loved her before she knew or loved God, somebody has to be there to tell her. Somebody has to believe the promise well enough to come to the child later and say, "You have been baptized, and here's what it means." The child can never discover this for herself but learns it as she is incorporated into the community.

Of course, we also have many adults coming into the church through Baptism. We also need opportunities for them to tell about how they were called by Jesus and what Baptism has meant for them in their continuing life of commitment to God and God's purposes.

Why do you think that this understanding of Baptism is especially needed in our time and our society?

In our society people's worth is often judged according to their economic contribution. Your worth is determined by what you're paid. Baptism teaches us that a person's worth is not governed by his or her work. Each person, young or old or middle-aged, is valuable as a redeemed child of God.

FOR GROUP DISCUSSION

If participants have not already read the chapter, allow some time for them to read it silently now or have parts of it read aloud.

Discuss one or more of the following questions. If your group is large, you may want to break down into groups of three or four.

1. What do you remember about your own baptism or from what others told you about it?

2. What does the fact that you were baptized mean to you?

3. How does the knowledge that you are baptized influence your life in your family? at your work or school? in your community?

4. How could your congregation help people understand and live out the daily meaning of their baptism?

5. Are there events in your life that tell you that God still comes to you?

6. Read the following quotations. How do they help you understand the meaning of your baptism?

> We must know what Baptism signifies and why God ordained just this sign and external observance for the sacrament by which we are first received into the Christian church. This act or observance consists in being dipped into the water, which covers us completely, and being drawn out again. These two parts, being dipped under the water and emerging from it, indicate the power and effect of Baptism, which is simply the slaying of the old Adam and the resurrection of the new man, both of which actions must continue in us our whole life long. Thus a Christian life is

nothing else than a daily Baptism, once begun and ever continued. For we must keep at it incessantly, always purging out whatever pertains to the old Adam, so that whatever belongs to the new man may come forth.[1]

That is the right use of Baptism among Christians, signaled by baptizing with water. Where this amendment of life does not take place but the old man is given free rein and continually grows stronger, Baptism is not being used but resisted. . . . On the other hand, when we become Christians, the old man daily decreases until he is finally destroyed. This is what it means to plunge into Baptism and daily come forth again.[2]

7. What did you find most interesting or helpful in this chapter?

You may want to close your group discussion by singing one of these hymns:

LBW 189 *We Know That Christ Is Raised*
LBW 192 *Baptized into Your Name Most Holy*
LBW 194 *All Who Believe and Are Baptized*
WOV 696 *I've Just Come from the Fountain*
WOV 697 *Wash, O God, Our Sons and Daughters*

Close with this or another prayer:

Almighty God, grant that we, who have been redeemed from the old life of sin by our baptism into the death and resurrection of your Son Jesus Christ may be renewed in your Holy Spirit to live in righteousness and true holiness; through Jesus Christ our Lord. [3]

3

AN HONEST FAITH
FOR THE UPS AND DOWNS
OF LIFE

MARTIN LUTHER SPOKE of the Christian life using the Latin phrase *simul justus et peccator*. The Christian is both saint and sinner. Even after we enter the new life in Christ, sin still has a hold on us that bothers us all the time. Sin is never gone from the Christian life, so there is always a lifelong struggle and the need for the daily dying and rising that we spoke of in connection with Baptism. It's the struggle St. Paul described when he said, "The good that I would I do not, and the evil that I would not, that I do."

This understanding is, I believe, more true to the actual experience of people than the approach that suggests we should always be on some "feel good" religious high. The "I'm OK, you're OK" approach tends to gloss over the real struggles people have and the cruel things we say and do to each other or the delusion that we should always get our own way. It's also a counterbalance to the assumption that if I am a Christian, my life will be totally different, that my external circumstances or internal state will be completely changed. This understanding of the Christian as saint and sinner is also an alternative to the New Age notion that we are already perfect or even already God.

The assurance of our baptism frees us to look at the dark side of ourselves. We can admit that side to ourselves and to others. We are not afraid of revealing our weaknesses because we believe there is a cure for our sin and shortcomings.

This understanding that we are both saint and sinner also means that we are not surprised when suffering comes into our lives. We do not expect to be free of suffering on this side of death. God never promised us a rose garden. Life is always marked by brokenness and failure and betrayal and death. We have not yet arrived, but God is working in the midst of our situation. The pain we experience can bring us closer to understanding the suffering of Christ and somehow sharing in that suffering. Paul wrote about this in Philippians 3:10:

> I want to know Christ and the power of his
> resurrection and the sharing of his sufferings
> by becoming like him in his death, if somehow
> I may attain the resurrection from the dead.

This doesn't mean that we shouldn't try to get rid of the suffering, but that God is there in the suffering. It also means that Christ shares the pain that we wittingly or unwittingly inflict on others.

Seeing ourselves as both saint and sinner also leads us to greater humility and self-criticism. In our personal relationships we look for our own part in any conflict. We look to see where our own selfishness or self-centeredness are part of the problem.

And with this understanding we may, as a church, be less inclined to speak with ultimate authority for God on all issues. Instead we encourage study and mutual conversation on complex issues, realizing that our own self-interest may cloud our perceptions. We recognize that not all truth may be on our side. We are not yet God, so our pronouncements must always be examined for self-interest and self-righteousness. But we are free to do that because we believe that our salvation does not depend on our being right.

So this understanding of ourselves as saint and sinner saves us from both despair and complacency. Undergirded by the assurance of God's mercy as sealed in our baptism, we can enter the struggle every day, renewed by the Spirit of God.

What difference does it make in your life that you see yourself as both saint and sinner?

As with our discussion of Baptism, it pushes me to examine myself daily, to ask for God's forgiveness, and for strength and guidance to carry out the tasks of each day.

One of the wonderful things about being at Luther College was the daily chapel service, which interrupted the decision making and strategic planning and alumni relations. There was a time for daily meditation on the life of faith. Before chapel would begin, I had time to lay before God some of the things I was working on, to ask for insight into my own selfishness or shortcomings, to ask for assistance. I found it to be a very good help in coping with my responsibilities. Often it didn't give me answers, but it gave me a chance to ask more questions and look at the issue from all sides. It certainly comforted me and strengthened me to keep at it, to go back. And then in the service itself there were prayers of confession and for guidance and strengthening.

Could this doctrine of simul justus et peccator be misused?

It's certainly misused if we succumb to what Dietrich Bonhoeffer called "cheap grace," if we continue sinning and say, "Well, that's just how things are," if we avoid the daily repentance and struggle with what's wrong in our lives.

It's also misused if we expect God to do it all. If the battle is going to be won in any sense, we have to enter the fray every day and do more than just expect God to knock down all our enemies. Instead, we encounter the evil in our own lives, ask forgiveness, and go on into the next day.

CHEAP GRACE IS THE DEADLY ENEMY of our Church. We are fighting today for costly grace. . . . Cheap grace means the justification of sin without the justification of the sinner. Grace alone does everything, they say, and so everything can remain as it was before. . . . Cheap grace is the preaching of forgiveness without requiring repentance, baptism without church discipline, Communion without confession, absolution without personal confession. Cheap grace is grace without discipleship, grace without the cross, grace without Jesus Christ, living and incarnate.[1]

—*Dietrich Bonhoeffer*

You have spoken of "God's long conversation with the soul." What do you mean by that?

God's relationship to each individual is not a trivial or once-and-for-all thing. God makes constant approaches to individuals, and sometimes we respond. There's an interchange with God that I call a conversation. God uses all sorts of experiences and people in our lives, not just preaching or church services. There are many other means that God uses to touch us.

What are some of the significant markers in God's long conversation with your soul?

My parents, of course, got me started. Then I had a very good pastor for confirmation, Robert Marshall. In college and seminary, there were professors who were very important to me. In my marriages I found partners who were spiritually challenging for me, sympathetic but also leading me to seek God in new ways.

These were some of the influential people, but there were also experiences in my life, not all of them happy. I had the usual doubts in college and then when my first wife died there were moments when God's conversation with my soul seemed faint. But I always believed that God was ready to resume the conversation.

Can you recall a time when your understanding of yourself as saint and sinner changed your relationship with another person?

In my marriage this idea is a constant help. When I get into a conflict, I recognize that here's a person whom I love saying, "It doesn't look the same way to me as it looks to you." Knowing I'm saint and sinner doesn't mean I'm half right and half wrong. I can be totally wrong, but God loves me still and gives me an opportunity to try again.

How might this idea of saint and sinner be beneficial in our society?

I think it can help us deal with the seemingly increasing polarization by race, by gender, by class. We recognize that the real division is not between us good guys and those other bad guys, but the line between good and evil is within the heart of each one of us. It helps us recognize that there's still sin in our own righteous position. If there's some opposition out there, it may be because of some blind spot, some terrible consequence, some barb in our own position that we're not taking account of or that is inflicting some kind of harm on others.

This doctrine also helps the church to be a little more modest about what it says, and it should help in trying to promote a climate of moral deliberation. It ought to provide a check on my own position in which I say, "Wait a minute. I really do need to hear what these other people are saying." There's likely to be more self-interest in what I say than I'm willing to admit. I always learn from the voice of the other.

So also in our church fights: if we do not start with recognizing our own sin and self-centeredness, we will only fall into that polarizing pattern that is the bane of our society.

How does this idea that we are both saint and sinner apply to the relationships between denominations?

The "ecumenical movement" is based on the principle that God's truth is bigger than our minds. We need to recognize that, good as our tradition is, it can always be enriched by listening to other Christian voices. It is certainly no diminishment of God's revelation to admit that we "know only in part" (1 Corinthians 13:12). That is why I am so heartened to see our church stretching itself to seek full communion with other denominations. We have much to offer each other. Just as some books of the New Testament are true but not complete-in-themselves witnesses to Jesus Christ, so our teaching of the faith can be augmented by others.

Paul taught that the reconciliation between Jews and Greeks in the Christian church was a sign to the world that God's plan was being accomplished (Ephesians 3:10). What a sign it would be to our quarrelsome and polarized generation if we could be reconciled with some of our sister denominations.

THIS LIFE IS NOT A BEING HOLY but a becoming holy; it is not a being well but a getting well; it is not a being but a becoming; it is not inactivity but practice. . . . As yet we are not what we ought to be, but we are getting there; the task is not yet accomplished and completed, but it is in progress and pursuit. The end has not yet been reached, but we are on the way that leads to it; as yet everything does not glow and sparkle, but everything is purifying itself.[2]

—*Martin Luther*

FOR GROUP DISCUSSION

If the group has not already read this chapter, give them some time to do so silently or have the chapter read aloud. Discuss one or more of the following questions. You may want to let the group choose which ones they want to discuss.

1. When we say that one of the purposes of the church is to bring people to faith, what do we really mean?

2. How do we expect this faith to influence their lives?

3. What things do we need to do better or differently in helping others to faith?

4. Do you ever feel this conflict of being *simul justus et peccator*, both saint and sinner, in your own life? How do you deal with it?

5. How might your own self-righteousness or self-interest influence your opinions on an issue like gun control or abortion?

6. How would you describe the story of God's long conversation with your soul? What have been the key markers? the high points? the low points?

7. What can we learn about the Christian life from these selections from the Lutheran Confessions of the Reformation period?

> It is also taught among us that such faith should produce good fruits and good works and that we must do all such good works as God has commanded, but we should do them for God's sake and not place our trust in them as if thereby to merit favor before God.[3]

> Penitence ought to produce good fruits. What these fruits are, we learn from the commandments—prayer, thanksgiving, the confession of the Gospel, the teaching of the Gospel, obedience to parents and magistrates, faithfulness to one's calling, peaceable conduct instead of

murder and hatred, the greatest possible generosity to the needy, restraint and chastisement of the flesh instead of adultery and fornication, truthfulness—not to buy off eternal punishment but to keep from surrendering to the devil or offending the Holy Spirit. These fruits are commanded by God, they should be done to his glory and because of his command, and they have their reward.[4]

8. What did you find most interesting or helpful in this chapter?

You may wish to celebrate your discussion by singing one of these hymns:

LBW 448 *Amazing Grace, How Sweet the Sound*
LBW 461 *Fight the Good Fight*
LBW 487 *Let Us Ever Walk with Jesus*
LBW 511 *Renew Me, O Eternal Light*
WOV 737 *There Is a Balm in Gilead*

✳

Close with this or another prayer:

> *Most merciful God, we confess that we are in*
> *bondage to sin and cannot free ourselves. We*
> *have sinned against you in thought, word,*
> *and deed, by what we have done and by what*
> *we have left undone. We have not loved you*
> *with our whole heart; we have not loved our*
> *neighbors as ourselves. For the sake of your*
> *Son, Jesus Christ, have mercy on us. Forgive*
> *us, renew us and lead us, so that we may*
> *delight in your will and walk in your ways,*
> *to the glory of your holy name. Amen.* [5]

4

CALLED TO BE SERVANTS

WHEN I WAS IN CONFIRMATION CLASS, our pastor not only taught us the catechism, but also tried to help us, as growing young people, to think about large questions such as what our vocation ought to be. He said we should always ask these questions:

1. What talents has God given me?
2. How can I use these gifts to help others?
3. How can I help the most people with these gifts?

Martin Luther taught that the Christian is "perfect lord of all, subject to none," and "perfect dutiful servant of all, subject to all." All Christians are called to serve God in the world.

This is a direct challenge to the privatism and the rampant consumerism that infect our society—the idea that I am responsible only for me and mine and that the satisfaction of my desires is a top priority. The very gifts God has given us require us to use them in service to our neighbors—in our families, our communities, the world.

This need not be a dismal burden. It can be a welcome message that a person is needed. People want to count for something. They want to find meaning in their lives. We can offer them that meaning. It is encouraging for all people to discover that they have talents that the world and the church can use.

God's creative activity is carried out in all the social structures of life—in the family, the economy, the government—not just in the church. This means that Christians are doing God's work all the time, not just when they're serving on the evangelism committee or church council.

I believe that we need to think creatively especially about two groups: the young and the old. They are the ones to whom our usual way of talking about vocation—as a job for pay, as a career—do not apply.

There is good news on the youth front. In my travels to synods around the country I have asked clergy and associates in ministry to tell me what signs of hope they are seeing in their work. I have been surprised at the number of times they have mentioned young people.

Young people? Aren't they supposed to be the big problem—not enough of them, not interested in the church, not willing to listen, and so forth?

The people who work with our youth tell a different story. They describe today's young people as more interested in service than in pizza and volleyball. They say there is a new seriousness out there. Our youth want to count for something. Young people want meaningful activity. They want to build houses for Habitat for Humanity or clean up youth camps in Slovakia.

At the other end of the spectrum are the older people, who are retiring early and have many years of active life ahead. When they get bored playing golf or rearranging furniture, they are open to the challenges that will use the expertise they have spent a lifetime acquiring.

All of us, whatever our age or position in life, can see ourselves as gifted children of God, with talents to use to accomplish good in the world.

A CHRISTIAN LIVES NOT IN HIMSELF, but in Christ and in his neighbor. Otherwise he is not a Christian. He lives in Christ through faith, in his neighbor through love. By faith he is caught up beyond himself into God. By love he descends beneath himself into his neighbor.[1]

—*Martin Luther*

Some women and members of minority groups caution us about the abuses of power that can be connected to the concept of servanthood, because they have experienced its being used to demean them and others. How might this concept be redeemed for them?

That's an important question. Jesus does call his disciples to be servants, and Paul talks about us as slaves of Jesus Christ. But this does not mean that a servant, or even a slave, does only menial tasks or degrading work. In Old Testament times, even in ancient Rome, slaves were often skilled persons who had been enslaved when their nation was conquered by an invading army. So physicians, craftsmen, goldsmiths, and others were slaves. To be a servant or a slave meant to have a skill but to use that skill for the good of others.

I heard a pastor say in a sermon, "The problem here is that people are so busy pursuing their careers that they have no time for ministry." Could you comment on that?

Well, I suppose he was just mad that people weren't doing some of the things around the church that needed to be done. But we have to see that the ministry of the laity is not limited to church work, nor is it just being an evangelist at our place of employment. It is doing the work itself.

I'm thinking of Bob's Standard station in Decorah, Iowa. Bob Usgaard is a fabulous guy. Although he is not an alumnus of Luther College, we gave him the alumni award that we give to one Decorah resident every year. We honored Bob not just because of his honesty and his willingness to employ students, but for his getting up on cold, icy mornings and starting cars, caring for people in that way.

Of course, there's another side to this question of serving in the congregation. You also have to ask yourself, "Am I committing myself so fully to working for my family and on my job that I have no time for church? Is the amount of time I'm spending on my family really for my family or is it to achieve a certain living standard that I aspire to but it means obsessive work far beyond what is healthy? Is my unwillingness to accept this task at church really because I don't have time, or is it simply a way of conveniently saying that I won't accept my responsibility to the fellowship?"

Much is said today about the demeaning nature of work in factories or fast-food restaurants or corporations. Is there some way the Christian understanding of vocation can help people to a more positive attitude?

First of all, we need to ask ourselves whether we can use this teaching about Christian vocation as a critique of work. So far as work does not contribute to the common good and does not itself enhance and support the personhood of the people doing it, it is not right. Just because people are doing what somebody else tells them to do does not mean that this is a Christian vocation or that they are being Christian servants. There is a challenge to the employer, as well as to the employee, to see to it that work somehow contributes to the health not only of the human race but also to those who are doing the work.

Does this suggest that there are some kinds of work that should not be done?

Yes, and I think of the gambling industry. If you're a dealer at a table, can this be a Christian vocation? You might be able to consider it a gift God has given you to provide for your family, but it might also be something you should be looking to replace with a different kind of job by using your earnings to educate yourself or maybe to move to another city.

We also need to rethink the whole way we involve people in the life of the church. Although people are saying they don't have time to do some things in church, this is because some of those things may not really need to be done. Pastors tell me that people are still interested in doing meaningful and significant work in the church.

What are some of the issues in our society that you think Christians need to respond to as servants of Christ?

Opportunities to reach across social and ethnic lines to work with people in other contexts are very important. Retired people delivering Meals on Wheels is one example. People work in soup kitchens. There are programs like the Stephen Ministry of South Central Illinois Synod. Prisons are being moved there, and the women of the churches have discovered a ministry in setting up centers to care for the families of inmates while they are visiting.

Another thing that's happening is that both younger people and older people are traveling overseas, and this gives great possibilities for bridging. By bridging I mean especially personal contact. That's the only life-changing way to meet people and help them.

Sometimes people are so overwhelmed by the problems in our society and in the world that they just become paralyzed. What resources do we have to overcome that despair?

We need to direct people to the spiritual resources of prayer and worship. I talked to a woman on the West Coast who spent time as a volunteer with Mother Teresa. She said that one can't do the kind of work Mother Teresa does without a regular community of prayer. One needs that strength to deal with the anger and complaining from those who are dying but who nevertheless are very human in their efforts to assert their own personhood.

We also can rely on the fact that we are part of the church and that the whole people of God have skills and resources far beyond individuals.

Think beyond our own body to others, like the Episcopalians and the Methodists and the Presbyterians; they have experience and skills in areas where Lutherans are weak.

The challenge becomes, How can we use this beautifully articulated family, this body of Christ? The issues are global, but the church is also global. We have the resources. We have tremendous opportunities to work together.

GOD DOES NOT WANT hearers and repeaters of words, but doers and followers who exercise themselves in the faith that worketh by love. For a faith that is without love is not enough—rather it is not faith at all, but a counterfeit of faith, just as a face seen in a mirror is not a real face, but merely the reflection of a face.[2]

—*Martin Luther*

FOR GROUP DISCUSSION

If the members of the group have not already read this chapter, give them an opportunity to do so now, or have the chapter read aloud. Discuss one or more of the following questions. If the group is large, you may want to break up into threes or fours.

1. What gifts or talents has God given you?

2. How can you use them in service to your family, your community, the world?

3. What can we do as employers or employees so that work enhances the well-being of the employee?

4. How can people find meaningful work to do in congregations?

5. If one of our purposes as a church is to respond to human need, what needs most demand a response from us?

6. Where can we have the greatest effect?

7. What means should we use?

8. How do you renew yourself for service in the world?

9. What did you find most interesting or helpful in this chapter?

You may wish to close your discussion by singing a hymn like one of these:

LBW 469 *Lord of All Hopefulness*
LBW 558 *Earth and All Stars!*
LBW 423 *Lord Whose Love in Humble Service*
WOV 765 *Jesu, Jesu, Fill Us with Your Love*
WOV 758 *Come to Us, Creative Spirit*

Close with this or another prayer:

Almighty God, your Son Jesus Christ dignified our labor by sharing our toil. Be with your people where they work; make those who carry on the industries and commerce of this land responsive to your will; and to all of us, give pride in what we do and a just return for our labor; through your Son, Jesus Christ our Lord. [3]

5

THE POWER OF THE GOSPEL

THIS IS A GOOD TIME to be the church. The collapse of all the structures that shored up the church and made it the center of the community now brings us an opportunity to rediscover the gospel as "the power of God" (Romans 1:16).

When we're challenged as a church, we are healthier than when we are not. It's just like exercise. When the doctor tells you to exercise, it's to help your body function the way it was meant to function. We have to ask ourselves whether the Christian church was meant to function as a soft, easy pillow or whether it was, from the beginning, a challenge to follow Christ, to take up a cross and follow, and in that following to discover the power of God. Difficulties and challenges throw us back on the mercies of God.

When everything's going well, it's easy to forget that God is good and that God has provided those blessings. When things get tough, our prayer life improves and our sensitivity to God's promptings and God's leadings becomes much more enhanced.

The awareness can also arise when we are challenged by tasks too big for us. When I was installed as bishop, I could answer yes to the questions Bishop Herbert Chilstrom put to me only by adding ". . . and I ask God to help me."

We fall back now on the power of the Word,

for it is the Word that builds the church. When I talk about the Word, I do not mean only preaching or Bible study. I mean the visible Word in the sacraments of Baptism and the Lord's Supper, the word spoken in pastoral care, the word we speak to one another, what Luther referred to as the "mutual conversation and consolation" of the brothers and sisters in Christ.

As we discover that the Christian message has power to address our needs and our sinful self-indulgence, it will enliven our ability to evangelize—to share this Word with others—because we will have seen the effect of God's Word. We will be able to say with the first disciples, "Lord, to whom shall we go? You have the words of eternal life."

I never saw this as a dogmatic statement but as the "bottom line" of seekers who had tried all the other solutions and found that only Jesus had words that held up.

I have always delighted in the account of the Samaritan woman in John 4 when she asks townsfolk, "This couldn't be the Christ, could it?" (the emphasis of the Greek text). And then, after the townsfolk have met Jesus, they declare to her, "This is the Christ, the Son of God." Her timid testimony returned to her as full-grown.

On this model, sharing the good news about Jesus is not a process of pouring my great faith into my faith-poor neighbor, but rather discovering that my imperfect faith can be used by God in a way that will surprise me—and thus be a faith-building experience. Perhaps this is part of what Paul meant by God's strength being made perfect in our weakness (2 Corinthians 12:9).

This power of the Word also reminds us of the truth claims of Christianity. Christianity is not just a convenient and comfortable way to live—an option among other lifestyles. It is the revelation of the way, the truth, and the life. It is therefore not at our beck and call, pliable to our needs, "there for us." It stands independent of our ability to grasp it all, to prove it, or accept it. It in fact judges us, calls into question our accommodations to "reality" and our insistence on our own way.

As I've visited around the church and talked with people, it's clear that several things alarm folks. One is that the United States is such a mobile country. People move from place to place and lose their roots—their roots in the faith. When people move, they don't automatically look for a church of the same denomination—or indeed for any church at all. The new situation gives them many new options, and they shop around. We may not like that, but it is one of the facts of life.

People also seem less rooted in the faith, less familiar with the traditions of the past. Their Bible knowledge seems to be very scanty. They have not been reared in the Bible stories, the life of faith, the way some of us were.

We can see this mobility as a positive thing. It means that people are ready to hear what we have to say. When they come to our churches, if they are welcomed and find a message of vitality and spiritual depth, they are ready to become part of a new tradition, even though they weren't raised that way.

We need to be a welcoming church so that when these seekers arrive at our door, we don't treat them as if they are aliens from another planet, but we help them understand the way we worship and how we draw on our traditions in our church and in our work.

We also need to be sure that the message we preach is, indeed, a Christ-centered message, because there are many other options out there in the world. We need to be sure that we are giving them what the church alone has to provide—not just a warm handshake and a cup of coffee, but the welcoming of God, the openness of God to their hurt, to their need, and the openness of God to challenge them to be Christ for their neighbor as well. That's a big job.

As pastors or lay people, even if you don't have personal prestige or public acclaim, you have a very powerful message, a means of change. You are not alone: the message you are bearing as a Christian has its own power, its own authenticity. Therefore you do not have to be a clever debater, you do not have to be the world's most brilliant theologian to speak a word of comfort and hope to your neighbor.

ALTHOUGH THE CHRISTIAN is thus free from all works, he ought in this liberty to empty himself, take upon himself the form of a servant, be made in the likeness of men, be found in human form, and to serve, help, and in every way deal with his neighbor as he sees that God through Christ has dealt and still deals with him. This he should do freely, having regard for nothing but divine approval. [1]

—*Martin Luther*

Why do you think that the fact that the church no longer sits at the center of our society may actually be a good thing?

Because there are so many corruptions and temptations and false gods associated with being in the center of society. One begins to see oneself as the ultimate and to depend on false power. This is really idolatry—taking a subordinate good and making it into an ultimate. So the church, by seeking to preserve its prestige and influence, may actually be guilty of idolatry.

In our day of so much cultural diversity, how do we still maintain the truth claims of Christianity?

In our contact with people of other religious traditions I think we should not say simply, "We have the truth, and we're going to teach you the truth." Instead we should come in and say, "Let us tell you about Jesus." We need to focus on the figure of Jesus and say, "Look at this person, his life, his words. This is what we are about," and start the dialogue at that point.

We used to see these other world religions as just idolatry. Now the tendency is to view them romantically as better than our own. The truth may be somewhere in between. Perhaps these religions have the potential for self-renewal and self-cleansing the way Christianity does. Perhaps it is even the contact with Christianity that will catalyze the process, and Christ will become the key for their renewal. This would be a surprising fulfillment of that statement: "No one comes to the Father but by me." Our task is to stay in contact and conversation with these religions, presenting what we know of Jesus as our contribution to their self-transformation. The rest is up to God.

How can more people in our church and communities be drawn into a study of the Word as we find it in the Bible?

That's a challenging question: How do you get the Word to people or into people? First of all, some people are vaccinated; they think they already know everything. So you need to break through to get them to hear with new ears. Second, with the bombardment of the media today, there's a lot of competition. And, third, some people talk loudly about the value of Bible study, but they don't seem to want to do it.

People also seek different benefits from Bible study. Some people want information; some want comfort; some come with specific questions (What does the Bible teach about this or that?); some come expecting to be surprised. There is no end to the possibilities. Our job is to begin where they are and then be good tour guides, leading them into new territory.

You spoke about making our worship services welcoming and meaningful to people. How can we do that?

It begins with the worship leaders. What do they expect? Is their happiest moment when they can say, "Thank heavens nothing happened today"? Do they approach worship with the anticipation that they—and the congregation—will meet God? It is even more awe-inspiring when we realize that in Holy Communion Jesus has promised to meet *us*. Here he comes, ready or not!

I think if pastors spent as much time working on the worship services as we spend on the sermons—or at least used to spend—that would make them more meaningful. If worship is to be meaningful, it has to be thought through—by the pastor, the church musicians, the worship committee, another group of lay persons. For some people, a very meaningful part of the Christian life could be thinking through the biblical texts for the particular Sunday and considering how their meaning might be enhanced for the whole congregation.

I think pastors or adult education leaders could also teach more about what we do and say in worship. Above all, we need to communicate a sense of reverence, a feeling of awe that we are coming into the presence of God.

FOR GROUP DISCUSSION

If your group has not already read the chapter, give them time to do so silently now, or have the chapter read aloud. Discuss one or more of the following questions. You may want to allow the group to choose which questions most interest them.

1. How has the Word been a power in your life?

2. What has been your best experience of offering a word of hope and comfort to someone in need?

3. What has been your experience with Bible study? What has worked best for you? Why?

4. In what ways could worship services of your congregation be made more welcoming and meaningful to congregation members and to seekers or visitors?

5. What did you find most interesting or helpful in this chapter?

6. How has this study and discussion helped you say, "This is a good time to be the church"?

✳

You may want to end your discussion by singing one of the following hymns:

LBW 240 *Father of Mercies, in Your Word*
LBW 227 *How Blest Are They Who Hear God's Word*
LBW 377 *Lift High the Cross*
LBW 369 *The Church's One Foundation*

✳

Close with this or another prayer:

> *Lord God of our salvation, it is your will that all people might come to you through your Son Jesus Christ. Inspire our witness to him, that all may know the power of his forgiveness and the hope of his resurrection. We pray in his name.* [2]

NOTES

CHAPTER ONE: A GOOD TIME TO BE THE CHURCH

1. *Lutheran Book of Worship*, p. 45.

CHAPTER TWO: WALKING IN NEWNESS OF LIFE

1. Martin Luther, from the *Large Catechism*.
2. *Book of Concord*, p. 445.
3. *Lutheran Book of Worship*, 47.

CHAPTER THREE: AN HONEST FAITH FOR THE UPS
AND DOWNS OF LIFE

1. Dietrich Bonhoeffer, *The Cost of Discipleship* (New York: Macmillan, 1963), pp. 45-47.
2. *What Luther Says*, vol. 1, p. 235.
3. Augsburg Confession, VI, *Book of Concord*, p. 32.
4. *Apology to the Augsburg Confession*, Article XIII, *Book of Concord*, p. 210.
5. *Lutheran Book of Worship*, p. 56.

CHAPTER FOUR: CALLED TO BE SERVANTS

1. Martin Luther, from *The Freedom of a Christian*.
2. Martin Luther, from the *Wittenberg Sermons*, vol. 2.
3. *Lutheran Book of Worship*, p. 44.

CHAPTER FIVE: THE POWER OF THE GOSPEL

1. Martin Luther, from *The Freedom of a Christian*.
2. *Lutheran Book of Worship*, p. 46.

ABOUT THE AUTHOR

THE REVEREND H. GEORGE ANDERSON was elected bishop of the Evangelical Lutheran Church in America on August 19, 1995, during the ELCA's fourth Churchwide Assembly, in Minneapolis, Minnesota.

A Phi Beta Kappa from Yale, Anderson earned graduate degrees from the University of Pennsylvania and the Lutheran Theological Seminary at Philadelphia, and is known as a translator and author of many works on Lutheran history.

At the time of his election, Anderson was president of Luther College, having served in that capacity from 1982 to 1995. Prior to his tenure at Luther, he was on the faculty of Lutheran Theological Southern Seminary in Columbia, South Carolina, and served as its president from 1970 to 1982.

ALSO OF INTEREST
TO ADULT STUDY GROUPS

NEW! **Inspire Bible Study Series**—an in-depth study of the living Word of God that explores each of the types of biblical literature—Torah, History, Wisdom, Prophetic, Gospels, Letters, and Apocalyptic—and opens readers' hearts and minds to the Spirit.

True Faith in the True God: An Introduction to Luther's Life and Thought, Hans Schwarz

The Gift of the Gospel: Basic Teachings of the Christian Faith, H. Gerard Knoche

Joseph: Eleven Bible Studies on Genesis, Claus Westermann

Nurturing Silence in a Noisy Heart: How to Find Inner Peace, Wayne E. Oates

Listening for God: Contemporary Literature and the Life of Faith, Volumes 1 & 2, Paula J. Carlson and Peter S. Hawkins

Intersections Small Group Series—for adults seeking a personal, Christ-centered small group Bible study.

At your bookstore or from Augsburg Fortress Publishers
800-328-4648